ESSENTIAL SONGS FOR

clarinet

Available for
FLUTE, CLARINET, ALTO SAX, TENOR SAX, TRUMPET,
HORN, TROMBONE, VIOLIN, VIOLA, CELLO

T0071545

ISBN 978-1-4234-5532-5

HAL•LEONARD®
CORPORATION

7777 W. BLUEMOUND RD. P.O. BOX 13819 MILWAUKEE, WI 53213

Visit Hal Leonard Online at
www.halleonard.com

CONTENTS

ALL SHOOK UP

CLARINET

Words and Music by OTIS BLACKWELL
and ELVIS PRESLEY

ALL THE WAY

from THE JOKER IS WILD

CLARINET

Words by SAMMY CAHN
Music by JAMES VEN HEUSEN

AND I LOVE HER

CLARINET

Words and Music by JOHN LENNON
and PAUL McCARTNEY

ANYONE CAN WHISTLE

from ANYONE CAN WHISTLE

Clarinet

Words and Music by
STEPHEN SONDHEIM

Slowly and tenderly

AUTUMN LEAVES

CLARINET

English lyrics by JOHNNY MERCER
French lyrics by JACQUES PREVERT
Music by JOSEPH KOSMA

BABY, I LOVE YOUR WAY

CLARINET

Words and Music by
PETER FRAMPTON

BACK AT ONE

CLARINET

Words and Music by
BRIAN McKNIGHT

BEAUTIFUL

CLARINET

Words and Music by
LINDA PERRY

Moderately slow

BECAUSE OF YOU

CLARINET

Words and Music by KELLY CLARKSON,
DAVID HODGES and BEN MOODY

BENNIE AND THE JETS

CLARINET

Words and Music by ELTON JOHN
and BERNIE TAUPIN

Slow Rock

To Coda ⊕

D.C. al Coda

CODA ⊕

BLESS THE BROKEN ROAD

CLARINET

Words and Music by MARCUS HUMMON,
BOBBY BOYD and JEFF HANNA

15

BORN FREE

from the Columbia Pictures' Release BORN FREE

Clarinet

Words by DON BLACK
Music by JOHN BARRY

BRING HIM HOME

from LES MISÉRABLES

Clarinet

Music by CLAUDE-MICHEL SCHÖNBERG
Lyrics by ALAIN BOUBLIL and HERBERT KRETZMER

BREATHE

CLARINET

Words and Music by HOLLY LAMAR
and STEPHANIE BENTLEY

BYE BYE LOVE

CLARINET

Words and Music by FELICE BRYANT
and BOUDLEAUX BRYANT

Moderately fast

CALIFORNIA GIRLS

Clarinet

Words and Music by BRIAN WILSON
and MIKE LOVE

CAN YOU FEEL THE LOVE TONIGHT

from Walt Disney Pictures' THE LION KING

CLARINET

Music by ELTON JOHN
Lyrics by TIM RICE

THE CHICKEN DANCE

CLARINET

By TERRY RENDALL
and WERNER THOMAS

CLIMB EV'RY MOUNTAIN
from THE SOUND OF MUSIC

Clarinet

Lyrics by OSCAR HAMMERSTEIN II
Music by RICHARD RODGERS

CRAZY LITTLE THING CALLED LOVE

CLARINET

Words and Music by
FREDDIE MERCURY

COMPLICATED

CLARINET

Words and Music by AVRIL LAVIGNE,
LAUREN CHRISTY, SCOTT SPOCK
and GRAHAM EDWARDS

CROCODILE ROCK

CLARINET

Words and Music by ELTON JOHN
and BERNIE TAUPIN

DANCING QUEEN

CLARINET

Words and Music by BENNY ANDERSSON,
BJORN ULVAEUS and STIG ANDERSON

DON'T KNOW WHY

CLARINET

Words and Music by
JESSE HARRIS

DREAM LOVER

CLARINET

Words and Music by
BOBBY DARIN

DROPS OF JUPITER
(Tell Me)

Clarinet

Words and Music by PAT MONAHAN,
JIMMY STAFFORD, ROB HOTCHKISS,
CHARLIE COLIN and SCOTT UNDERWOOD

33

DUST IN THE WIND

CLARINET

Words and Music by
KERRY LIVGREN

EASTER PARADE

from AS THOUSANDS CHEER

CLARINET

Words and Music by
IRVING BERLIN

ENDLESS LOVE

CLARINET

Words and Music by
LIONEL RICHIE

FEVER

Clarinet

Words and Music by JOHN DAVENPORT
and EDDIE COOLEY

FIRE AND RAIN

CLARINET

Words and Music by
JAMES TAYLOR

THE FIRST CUT IS THE DEEPEST

CLARINET

Words and Music by
CAT STEVENS

THE FOOL ON THE HILL

CLARINET

Words and Music by JOHN LENNON
and PAUL McCARTNEY

FOOTLOOSE
Theme from the Paramount Motion Picture FOOTLOOSE

CLARINET

Words by DEAN PITCHFORD
and KENNY LOGGINS
Music by KENNY LOGGINS

FROM A DISTANCE

CLARINET

Words and Music by
JULIE GOLD

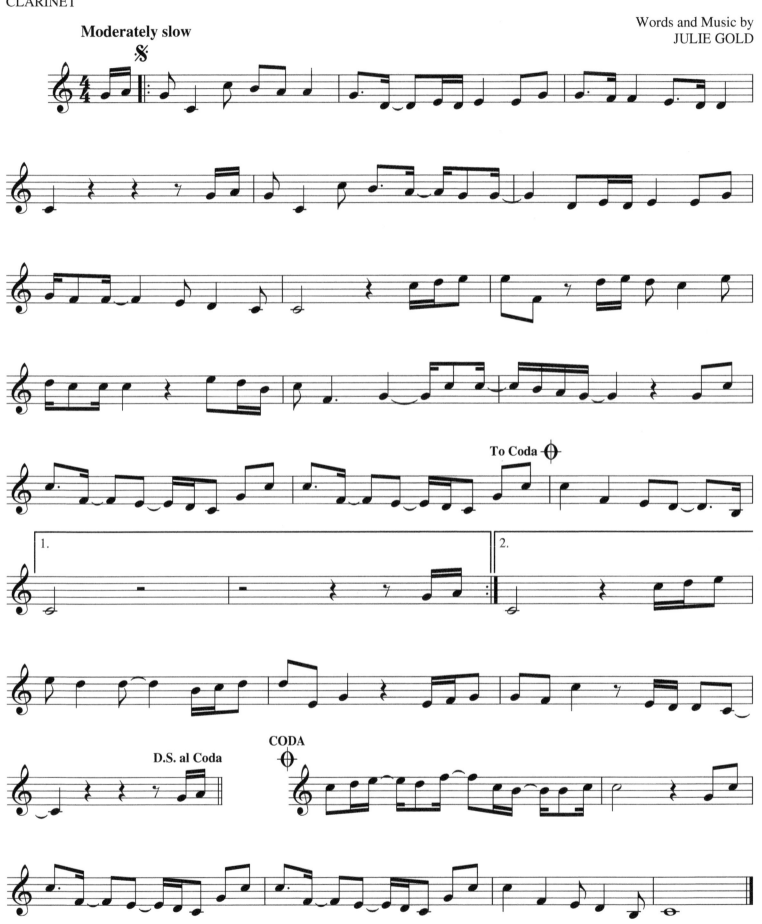

GO AWAY, LITTLE GIRL

CLARINET

Words and Music by GERRY GOFFIN
and CAROLE KING

GOOD VIBRATIONS

CLARINET

Words and Music by BRIAN WILSON
and MIKE LOVE

GOT MY MIND SET ON YOU

CLARINET

Words and Music by
RUDY CLARK

A GROOVY KIND OF LOVE

CLARINET

Words and Music by TONI WINE
and CAROLE BAYER SAGER

Moderately slow

HAPPY TOGETHER

CLARINET

Words and Music by GARRY BONNER
and ALAN GORDON

HAPPY TRAILS

from the Television Series THE ROY ROGERS SHOW

Clarinet

Words and Music by
DALE EVANS

HEAVEN

CLARINET

Words and Music by BRYAN ADAMS
and JIM VALLANCE

Copyright © 1983 IRVING MUSIC, INC., ADAMS COMMUNICATIONS, INC., ALMO MUSIC CORP. and TESTATYME MUSIC
All Rights for ADAMS COMMUNICATIONS, INC. Controlled and Administered by IRVING MUSIC, INC.
All Rights for TESTATYME MUSIC Controlled and Administered by ALMO MUSIC CORP.
All Rights Reserved   Used by Permission

HEAVEN

CLARINET

Words and Music by HENRY GARZA,
JOEY GARZA and RINGO GARZA

HELLO

CLARINET

Words and Music by
LIONEL RICHIE

HIGH HOPES

CLARINET

Words by SAMMY CAHN
Music by JAMES VAN HEUSEN

Moderately, with a beat

HOW CAN YOU MEND A BROKEN HEART

CLARINET

Words and Music by BARRY GIBB
and ROBIN GIBB

HOW SWEET IT IS (TO BE LOVED BY YOU)

CLARINET

Words and Music by EDWARD HOLLAND,
LAMONT DOZIER and BRIAN HOLLAND

I GOT YOU
(I Feel Good)

CLARINET

Words and Music by
JAMES BROWN

(Spoken:) Hey!

I HOPE YOU DANCE

CLARINET

Words and Music by TIA SILLERS
and MARK D. SANDERS

Moderately

I JUST CALLED TO SAY I LOVE YOU

CLARINET

Words and Music by
STEVIE WONDER

I LEFT MY HEART IN SAN FRANCISCO

CLARINET

Words by DOUGLASS CROSS
Music by GEORGE CORY

Moderately

I SHOT THE SHERIFF

CLARINET

Words and Music by
BOB MARLEY

I WANT TO HOLD YOUR HAND

CLARINET

Words and Music by JOHN LENNON
PAUL McCARTNEY

I'LL BE THERE

CLARINET

Words and Music by BERRY GORDY,
HAL DAVIS, WILLIE HUTCH
and BOB WEST

Moderately

I'LL BE

CLARINET

Words and Music by
EDWIN McCAIN

I'M WITH YOU

CLARINET

Words and Music by AVRIL LAVIGNE, LAUREN CHRISTY,
SCOTT SPOCK and GRAHAM EDWARDS

IF

CLARINET

Words and Music by
DAVID GATES

IF I HAD A HAMMER
(The Hammer Song)

Clarinet

Words and Music by LEE HAYS
and PETE SEEGER

THE IMPRESSION THAT I GET

CLARINET

Words and Music by DICKY BARRETT
and JOE GITTLEMAN

IN THE MOOD

CLARINET

By JOE GARLAND

IT'S A SMALL WORLD

from "it's a small world" at Disneyland Park and Magic Kingdom Park

CLARINET

Words and Music by RICHARD M. SHERMAN
and ROBERT B. SHERMAN

IT'S TOO LATE

CLARINET

Words and Music by CAROLE KING
and TONI STERN

ITSY BITSY TEENIE WEENIE
YELLOW POLKADOT BIKINI

CLARINET

Words and Music by PAUL VANCE
and LEE POCKRISS

THEME FROM "JURASSIC PARK"

from the Universal Motion Picture JURASSIC PARK

Clarinet

Composed by
JOHN WILLIAMS

KING OF THE ROAD

CLARINET

Words and Music by
ROGER MILLER

LA BAMBA

Clarinet

By RITCHIE VALENS

LET IT BE

CLARINET

Words and Music by JOHN LENNON
PAUL McCARTNEY

LISTEN TO WHAT THE MAN SAID

CLARINET

Words and Music by
PAUL and LINDA McCARTNEY

THE LOCO-MOTION

CLARINET

Words and Music by GERRY GOFFIN
and CAROLE KING

LOUIE, LOUIE

CLARINET

Words and Music by
RICHARD BERRY

LOVE ME TENDER

CLARINET

Words and Music by ELVIS PRESLEY
and VERA MATSON

LUCY IN THE SKY WITH DIAMONDS

CLARINET

Words and Music by JOHN LENNON
and PAUL McCARTNEY

MAMBO NO. 5
(A Little Bit Of...)

Clarinet

Original Music by DAMASO PEREZ PRADO
Words by LOU BEGA and ZIPPY

ME AND BOBBY McGEE

CLARINET

Words and Music by KRIS KRISTOFFERSON
and FRED FOSTER

A MOMENT LIKE THIS

CLARINET

Words and Music by JOHN REID
and JORGEN KJELL ELOFSSON

MY FAVORITE THINGS

from THE SOUND OF MUSIC

Clarinet

Lyrics by OSCAR HAMMERSTEIN II
Music by RICHARD RODGERS

THE ODD COUPLE

Theme from the Paramount Picture THE ODD COUPLE
Theme from the Paramount Television Series THE ODD COUPLE

Clarinet

By NEAL HEFTI

ON TOP OF SPAGHETTI

CLARINET

Words and Music by
TOM GLAZER

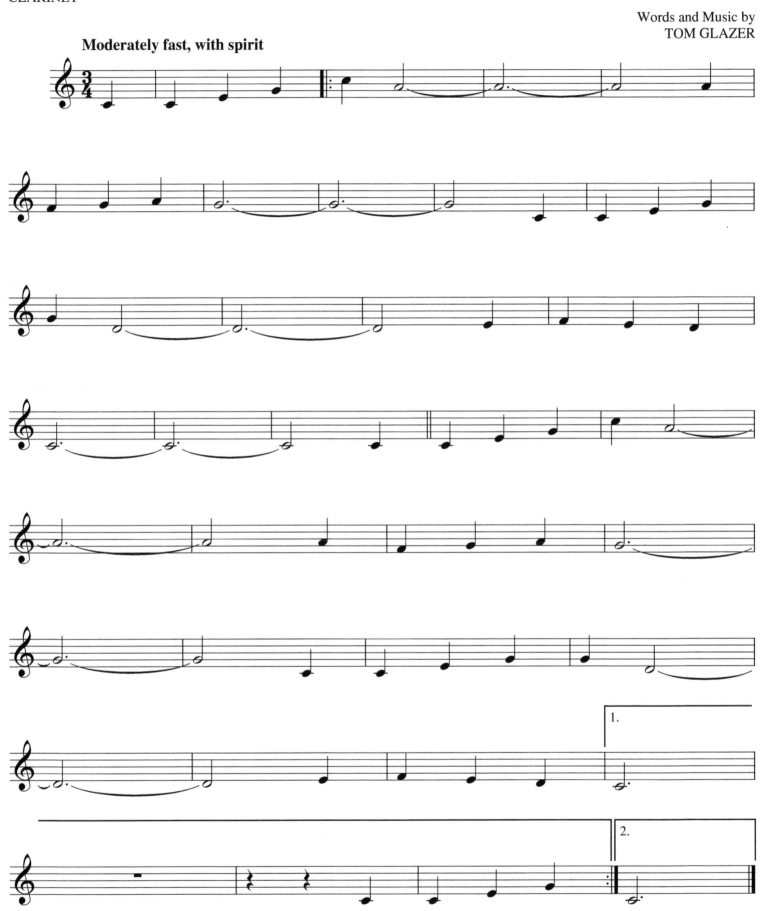

100 YEARS

CLARINET

Words and Music by
JOHN ONDRASIK

ONE NOTE SAMBA
(Samba de uma nota so)

CLARINET

Original Lyrics by NEWTON MENDONCA
English Lyrics by ANTONIO CARLOS JOBIM
Music by ANTONIO CARLOS JOBIM

Samba

PETER COTTONTAIL

CLARINET

Words and Music by STEVE NELSON
and JACK ROLLINS

PUPPY LOVE

CLARINET

Words and Music by
PAUL ANKA

QUE SERA, SERA
(Whatever Will Be, Will Be)
from THE MAN WHO KNEW TOO MUCH

Clarinet

Words and Music by JAY LIVINGSTON
and RAY EVANS

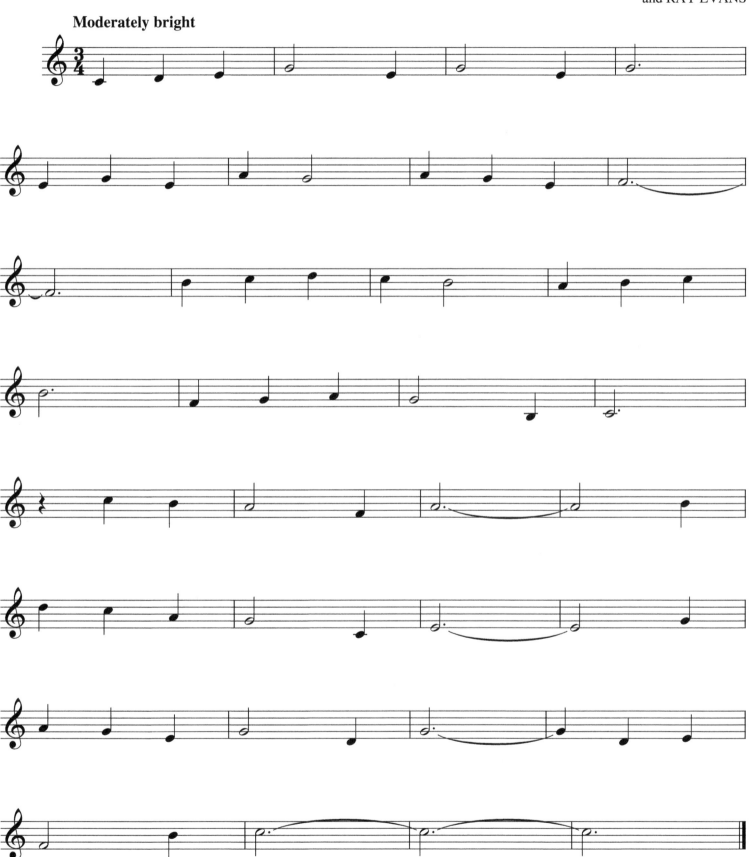

R.O.C.K. IN THE U.S.A
(A Salute to 60's Rock)

CLARINET

Words and Music by
JOHN MELLENCAMP

THE RAINBOW CONNECTION
from THE MUPPET MOVIE

CLARINET

Words and Music by PAUL WILLIAMS
and KENNETH L. ASCHER

RAINDROPS KEEP FALLIN' ON MY HEAD

from BUTCH CASSIDY AND THE SUNDANCE KID

Clarinet

Lyric by HAL DAVID
Music by BURT BACHARACH

ROCKIN' ROBIN

CLARINET

Words and Music by
J. THOMAS

SAILING

CLARINET

Words and Music by
CHRISTOPHER CROSS

SEE YOU LATER, ALLIGATOR

CLARINET

Words and Music by
ROBERT GUIDRY

SEVENTY SIX TROMBONES

from Meredith Willson's THE MUSIC MAN

CLARINET

By MEREDITH WILLSON

SHAKE, RATTLE AND ROLL

CLARINET

Words and Music by
CHARLES CALHOUN

SHOUT

CLARINET

Words and Music by ROLAND ORZABAL
and IAN STANLEY

SIXTEEN GOING ON SEVENTEEN

from THE SOUND OF MUSIC

Clarinet

Lyrics by OSCAR HAMMERSTEIN II
Music by RICHARD RODGERS

Slowly, with expression

SMOOTH

CLARINET

Words by ROB THOMAS
Music by ROB THOMAS and ITALL SHUR

SO NICE
(Summer Samba)

CLARINET

Original Words and Music by MARCOS VALLE
and PAULO SERGIO VALLE
English Words by NORMAN GIMBEL

Moderately

THE SOUND OF MUSIC
from THE SOUND OF MUSIC

Clarinet

Lyrics by OSCAR HAMMERSTEIN II
Music by RICHARD RODGERS

SPINNING WHEEL

CLARINET

Words and Music by
DAVID CLAYTON THOMAS

Funky, moderate Rock

SPLISH SPLASH

Clarinet

Words and Music by BOBBY DARIN
and MURRAY KAUFMAN

With a beat

STAND BY ME

CLARINET

Words and Music by JERRY LEIBER,
MIKE STOLLER and BEN E. KING

SUNNY

Clarinet

Words and Music by
BOBBY HEBB

Moderate Rock

SUPERCALIFRAGILISTICEXPIALIDOCIOUS

from Walt Disney's MARY POPPINS

CLARINET

Words and Music by RICHARD M. SHERMAN
and ROBERT B. SHERMAN

SURFIN' U.S.A.

CLARINET

Words and Music by
CHUCK BERRY

TAKIN' CARE OF BUSINESS

CLARINET

Words and Music by
RANDY BACHMAN

TEARS IN HEAVEN

CLARINET

Words and Music by ERIC CLAPTON
and WILL JENNINGS

TENNESSEE WALTZ

CLARINET

Words and Music by REDD STEWART
and PEE WEE KING

THAT'LL BE THE DAY

Clarinet

Words and Music by JERRY ALLISON,
NORMAN PETTY and BUDDY HOLLY

THIS LOVE

CLARINET

Words and Music by ADAM LEVINE
and JESSE CARMICHAEL

TIE A YELLOW RIBBON
ROUND THE OLE OAK TREE

CLARINET

Words and Music by L. RUSSELL BROWN
and IRWIN LEVINE

Moderately bright

TIJUANA TAXI

CLARINET

Words by JOHNNY FLAMINGO
Music by ERVAN "BUD" COLEMAN

TRUE COLORS

CLARINET

Words and Music by BILLY STEINBERG
and TOM KELLY

THE TWIST

CLARINET

Words and Music by
HANK BALLARD

UP WHERE WE BELONG

from the Paramount Picture AN OFFICER AND A GENTLEMAN

CLARINET

Words by WILL JENNINGS
Music by BUFFY SAINTE-MARIE and JACK NITZSCHE

WALKING IN MEMPHIS

CLARINET

Words and Music by
MARC COHN

THE WAY YOU LOOK TONIGHT
from SWING TIME

Clarinet

Words by DOROTHY FIELDS
Music by JEROME KERN

WE ARE FAMILY

Clarinet

Words and Music by NILE RODGERS
and BERNARD EDWARDS

WE ARE THE CHAMPIONS

CLARINET

Words and Music by
FREDDIE MERCURY

WE BUILT THIS CITY

CLARINET

Words and Music by BERNIE TAUPIN, MARTIN PAGE,
DENNIS LAMBERT and PETER WOLF

WE'VE ONLY JUST BEGUN

CLARINET

Words and Music by ROGER NICHOLS
and PAUL WILLIAMS

WHITE FLAG

CLARINET

Words and Music by RICK NOWELS,
ROLLO ARMSTRONG and DIDO ARMSTRONG

A WHOLE NEW WORLD

from Walt Disney's ALADDIN

CLARINET

Music by ALAN MENKEN
Lyrics by TIM RICE

Y.M.C.A.

CLARINET

Words and Music by JACQUES MORALI,
HENRI BELOLO and VICTOR WILLIS

YESTERDAY

CLARINET

Words and Music by JOHN LENNON
and PAUL McCARTNEY

Moderately, with expression

YOU ARE MY SUNSHINE

CLARINET

Words and Music by
JIMMIE DAVIS

YOU LIGHT UP MY LIFE

CLARINET

Words and Music by
JOSEPH BROOKS

YOU ARE THE MUSIC IN ME

CLARINET

from the Disney Channel Original Movie HIGH SCHOOL MUSICAL 2

Words and Music by
JAMIE HOUSTON

Moderately fast Rock

YOU'RE BEAUTIFUL

CLARINET

Words and Music by JAMES BLUNT,
SACHA SKARBEK and AMANDA GHOST

YOU'RE STILL THE ONE

Clarinet

Words and Music by SHANIA TWAIN
and ROBERT JOHN LANGE

YOU'VE GOT A FRIEND IN ME

from Walt Disney's TOY STORY

CLARINET

Music and Lyrics by
RANDY NEWMAN

YOUR SONG

Clarinet

Words and Music by ELTON JOHN
and BERNIE TAUPIN

ZOOT SUIT RIOT

CLARINET

Words and Music by
STEVE PERRY

Spoken: Blow, dad - dy!